The Butterfly Experience: Vol 1

A Collection of Poems
by
Kesha L Johnson-Clark
(~friscourbancowgrrl~)

ISBN: 0615620450
ISBN-13: 9780615620459

DEDICATION

Find solace in what means most to you and never jeopardize your sanity ...thank you.

-Kesha

1/24/10

ACKNOWLEDGMENTS

This book was created and formatted with the intent to distribute as published via Brown Sugar Promotions LLC in January 2010. The cover and cover art are credited to CreateSpace where applicable with the pre-assigned ISBN of 9781452816852. All content within this book and all corresponding copyrights are furnished via Brown Sugar Promotions LLC http://brwonsugarpromotionsllc.blogspot.com as ownership to the original author Kesha L Johnson-Clark (~friscourbancowgrrl~)

frebrurary skies

i want you here/next to me/lying with me/inside of me/there is no need to speak/for there is nothing more for either one of us to say/we both know of each other's mistakes/for it is you and only you that i am thinking of/dreaming of/wishing for/yearning for/crying for/for it is you and only you that i'd lie for/it is you and only you that i'd die for/it is your touch/your kiss/your shape/your love/i'd like to carve you in stone/so that i can have you forever/your scent/your taste/should be bottled and stored in a secret place/your words/your thoughts are of gold/just like mine/and for this/i know/what we have is purely divine

temporary paradise

was it you/or was it me/who started and ended us/so suddenly that rainy day/my heart is not broken/long before you/another carved his name/into that now hollow part of me/maybe i should cry but the tears never come/i have nothing but wide open desert/the harsh/dry words/escape from/your tongue/and i want to crush you/i want to erase you/i want to forget you and the love that plays/forever in my mind/and to form the words/i hate you is painful and i cannot remember/the last time/i felt so alone finding my way

i feel as though/the sun is shining/high and bright upon my soul/no longer am i afraid of the unknown/i welcome change and embrace the new possibilities/my wings have grown/i'm learning to fly/and soon i will soar high above the clouds until i've passed the stars/i will fly high until i burst open with happiness/my wings have grown and i no longer feel as though i am alone

closer to you

here we are/alone in silence/the heat our bodies create together /is limitless/if there were no tomorrow i would be/completely satisfied/with this moment/being my last/taste of living/you opened my mind/to the possibilities of what was/of what is and what could be/you are the newness that never gets old/tired or worn/you protect me/from myself/and i know your fears/and i can silence the screams/we are karma manifested/we are truth/we are more than we were the day before

caution

is it possible/could it be/you're thinking/guessing/wondering/how it would be/you and me/sexually/your eyes/can see through me/and i must admit/when we speak on the phone/i want to tell you/how i feel/but you'd probably think/i wasn't for real/ i must admit/i've wanted you for a while/i knew that it was best/to keep it to myself/i call you/my little wonder boy/i know that you're curious/don't try to deny/you want to know/what it feels like/inside/i see you/watching/my breast/hips/and thighs/and see/i know/you're gonna fall/you'll want to/make me your home/and i'll remember/how you/proceeded to know me/with caution/and how time even/you were/and how we/tried to hide/our passion/full and loud/so clear/anyone/miles away could hear the afterglow

i didn't realize it/at first/and now i'm knowing/that i hurt you/it wasn't supposed/to be that way/you and i/too scared to fall/i didn't realize it/at first/and now i'm knowing/that you love me/my beauty/my essence/i want/to share it/all with you/no more lies/no more cries/no more fucking around/with other guys/i didn't realize it/at first/and now i'm knowing/that i hurt you/i was wrong/you know me/the good/the bad/can you/love me now/will you/love me now/after everything/i apologize/to you/i didn't realize it/at first/and now i'm knowing

agenda

we are in a time/where things are more urgent than ever/the worlds agenda is changing/with the birth of each day/morning/noon/and night/people pray to their gods/asking to spare their lives/for another day/week/month or year/but i wonder if they hear/i wonder what will become of those/when our judgment day is near/feeling hearts and minds with such fear/for no one has led a life without sin/all minds wander into the dark/hollow places/revenge/each child that is born/will travel down that path/of uncertainty/guilt/despise/those who harmed their ancestors/learning to love/learning to trust/all born with dark hearts/learning to share/learning to care/joining as one race of people/with a common goal/to unite/this is the agenda of a new world/one common goal/to unite/no more hate/crime/prejudice/no more lying politicians/people dying in vain/material gain/no more broken promises/families torn apart/the agenda for the new world is smart/caring/full of love/balance and equality to start/support those who can not help themselves/this is the agenda/this is urgent/listen

for you

when we make love/ i escape from the pains/ the dullness/ the faded
lights and still life paintings of past lovers/i want to swallow you between
my thighs and release you into the day/exploring the unknown and
rediscovering the old and familiar/forming us/we/even three/i want to
bare sons and daughters for you/when we kiss/it's like a love song playing
forever in my mind/pressing rewind/forward/then stop/pausing at the
part when i scream your name/and i become high/intoxicated/breathing
you into my soul/i want to be everything for you/i want to be something
honest and pure/i want to be beautiful for you

raw

it was good/it was fast/it was deep/continuing strong/slowly becoming warmth/creating something only for you and i to keep/your love is like a razor blade/my love is like a hand granade/together we are toxic/i want you to know me/from the inside

seething

at times/i long to be/without the daily bullshit/noise of the city/the continuous talk of nothingness/the unimportant commonalities/the fake smiles/twisted/faces hidden/souls burning/everyone writing/their books on religion/preaching about the right path/but who knows for sure/for i want to go my own way/forget the maps/the tour guides/spirits travel/sometimes we need/to be lost for us/to really know where/we want to go/now i can see/the light shining bright

ascend

i am still/silent/taking in/my surroundings/smelling fear/even death/i see them/those with velvet lips/suicide kisses/those with dark hearts/closed minds/tainted spirits/i hear them/the lies/the cries/whispering/i welcome the night/shadows/dancing upon graves/returning to/that familiar place/high above/the clouds/into the light

check mate

there are times/when i look/at you/and i can truly see/what a
blessing/you are in my life/i know/that you are real/i
understand/happiness/peace/fulfillment/and joy/but then/there are
times/when i look/at you/through tearful eyes/with a broken heart/and i
know sadness/pain/and regret/and i know/the meaning of hope/so here i
am/looking at you/waiting...

hellbound

i hear souls crying/at night as i lay in bed from the untimely heat/the demons are gathering for prey/a song of sin and guilt/plays loud and clear for all to hear/the constant toll of bells/keep me reminded/that the fires will consume me as well

rogue

have you ever felt love/that explosion of emotions/deep down inside/the burning that keeps you awake at night/the thought that brings pleasure/every time that you touch/kisses of blackberry and gin/flowers in spring/warm nights in winter/like a porn movie star/fantasies become reality/up then down/back then forth/wet then dry/and wet again/becoming one/joined/creating the newness/have you ever felt love

sour

where do i began/how can i go on/i thought i knew the answers to the questions/but i was wrong/i see/babies crying/mothers sighing/father dying/where is the family/the house is gone/i see/no food to eat/no money for keep/how can i go on/i can't see tomorrow/yesterday is gone/we have only today/here/now/this moment

purge

bring me night/bring me death/sanity is not contained/purity is not holy/angels cry/demons watch/the smell/burning flesh/blood flows/the screams are numbing/my soul changes/with the moon/you can have/what's left of me

drugstore romeo

because you/could never satisfy/my need to be/seen as something
more/than human/something more than/flesh and bone/the eternal
wondering/has become overbearing/and i want to/taste freedom/i want
to seize the day/and explore untamed nights of passion/endless
pleasure/for i have/ high hopes and yet waiting/for you is/a destiny i will
not claim

the irony of it all

every now and then/i look inside/my soul/finding it full/of emptiness and pain/trust/when i say/that my heart/beats for you/and all that you are/loving you/is like being/in that cold and dark place/being alone/feeling as though/i've lost/a huge/part of me/searching/wanting/to fill that void/once/belonging to you

paper dolls

hearing the voices/seeing the faces/all unfamiliar/all lurking/hiding in the dark/waiting/to attack/when you've turned your back/laughing/smiling/not wanting/their masks to disappear/all of them/lying/pretending to care/as if you/were never there neurotic/erotic

i can't/i won't/stop this spinning/it is the sound/of your voice/the constant beating/of your heart/next to mine/it is the way/you look at me/through troubled eyes/testing my trust/forgiveness/and loyalty/this very moment/is my everlasting desire/twisting you/into the shape/i crave most

the honeymoon suite

the sun sets/palm trees/lavish lakes and white sand/laughter/the cool breeze/secrets unfold/our bodies/tingle from the wine/this day is truly divine/i belong to you/and you are mine/this is our celebration/gently caressing each other/with chocolate kisses/we dissolve/an eternal flame

stars

before you/there was another/i loved so deep/he touched my soul/he lived within/for he could not be erased/and though i promised/to share this life/we lost each other/now/i have you/i am at peace/this here/our love is soft/this here/our love is loud/this here/our love is proud/this here/with you/is my perfection/i am content/this here/total satisfaction/let us float

feelings

there are times/when this man drives me wild/has me craving long hot/sweaty nights/dreaming of passion fruit kisses/giving my all/not wanting the rush to stop/then there are those times/when he makes me want to rip his heart out/snatch the cat back/curse his name/burn his soul/and do all sorts of other unholy things to his flesh/but here i am today/full of grace/love/compassion/wanting more and more/to spend the rest of my life with this one man/he brightens my days and comforts my nights/warming my heart with each word that he speaks/each touch that he gives

angel: a song for the fallen

chorus: i'll be your angel/it doesn't matter/when you call/i'll be with you/through it all/i'll be your angel

verse 1: the pain is real/and cuts deep inside/and you start/to question why/you should even try/but your life/is worth living/it's not your time/to die

chorus: i'll be you angel/it doesn't matter/when you call/'ll be with you/through it all/i'll be your angel

verse 2: i know things/are kinda rough/and it all seems/like too much/you close your eyes/and start to cry/just remember/i'm by your side

chorus: i'll be you angel/it doesn't matter/when you call/i'll be with you/through it all/i'll be your angel

bridge: the days/are long/and the nights/are cold/but hold on/to what matters most/time is moving fast/and you can't undo/the past/I'm here/we're all here/with enough love/to last/trust it will last

chorus: i'll be your angel/it doesn't matter/when you call/i'll be with you/through it all/i'll be your angel

repeat chorus 4x

Submit all inquiries for this book to:

Brown Sugar Promotions LLC, A Publishing Imprint

Attn: Publishing, Licensing & Copyrights

P.O. Box 640281

San Francisco, California 94164

info@brownsugarpromotions.com

ABOUT THE AUTHOR

Kesha L Johnson-Clark (~friscourbancowgrrl~) has published titles with Brown Sugar
Promotions LLC, A Publishing Imprint since 2010

View her Amazon Author Page here http://amazon.com/author/keshajohnsonclark

View some of her select poems here http://www.poetfreak.com/poet/KeshaLJohnsonClark

Follow her Facebook Fan Page here http://www.facebook.com/KeshaLJohnsonClark

www.ingramcontent.com/pod-product-compliance
Lightning Source LLC
Chambersburg PA
CBHW041548040426
42447CB00002B/94